Animals Move

HEINLE
CENGAGE Learning

Y|S|G
A YBM COMPANY
Young & Son
Global, Inc.

How does your pet move?

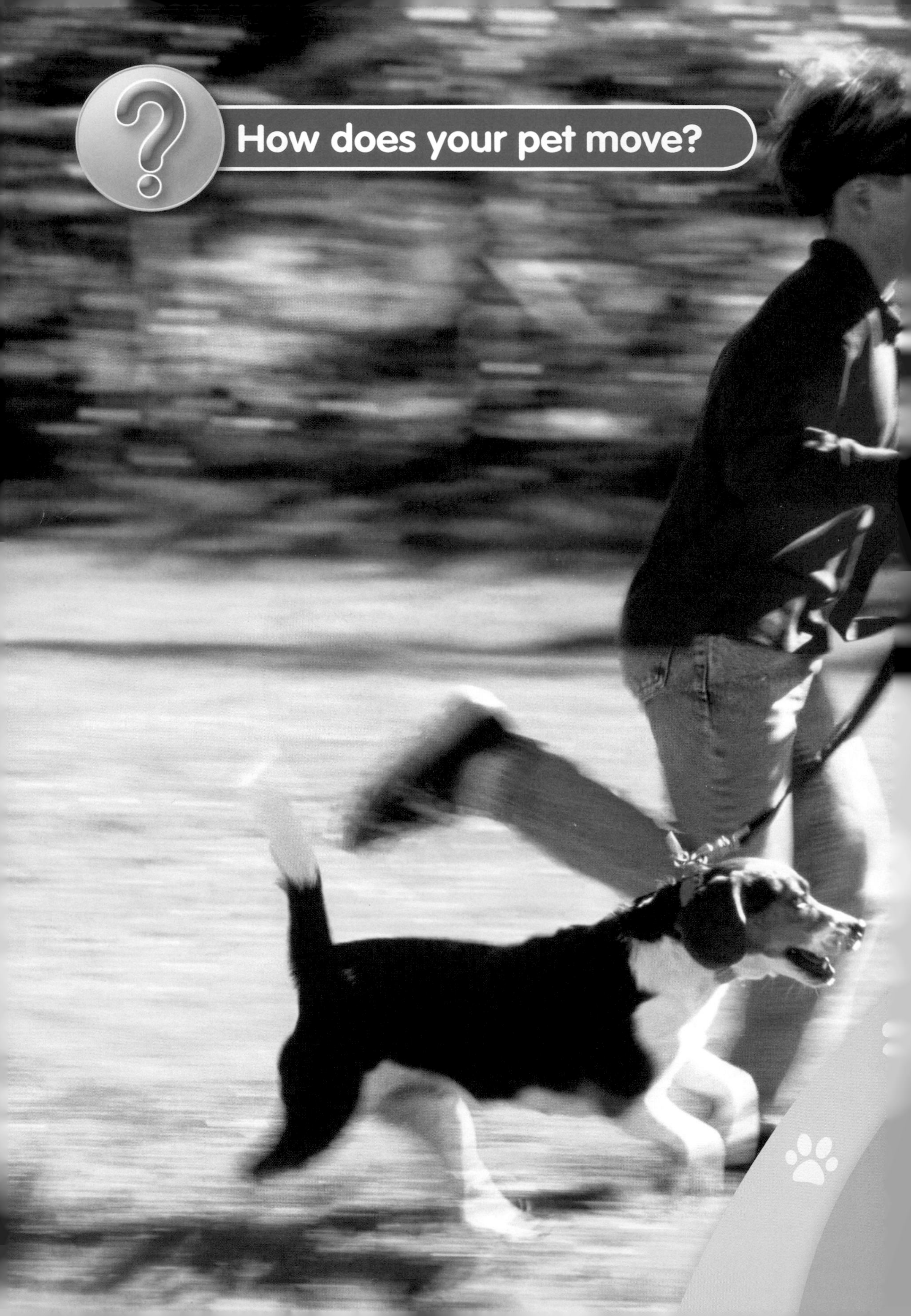

Contents

hop

run

jump

swing

swim

fly

Animals move in different ways.
Animals use their body parts
to move.

legs

A kangaroo has legs.
A kangaroo hops with its legs.

A cheetah has legs, too.
A cheetah runs with its legs.

A frog has legs, too.
A frog jumps with its legs.

arms

An orangutan has arms.
An orangutan swings with its arms.

fins

A dolphin has fins.
A dolphin swims with its fins.

An eagle has wings.
An eagle flies with its wings.

wings

How do these animals move?

How Do Animals Move?

Look at the animals. How do they move?
Cheetahs run, and kangaroos hop.
Frogs jump, and orangutans swing.
How about eagles and dolphins?

Look at the animals. How do they move?
Cheetahs run, and kangaroos hop.
Frogs jump, and orangutans swing.
How about eagles and dolphins?

Index